Reading Level 4.2
Points 1

05/09 Bound To Stay Bound $12.12